NUCLEAR POWER

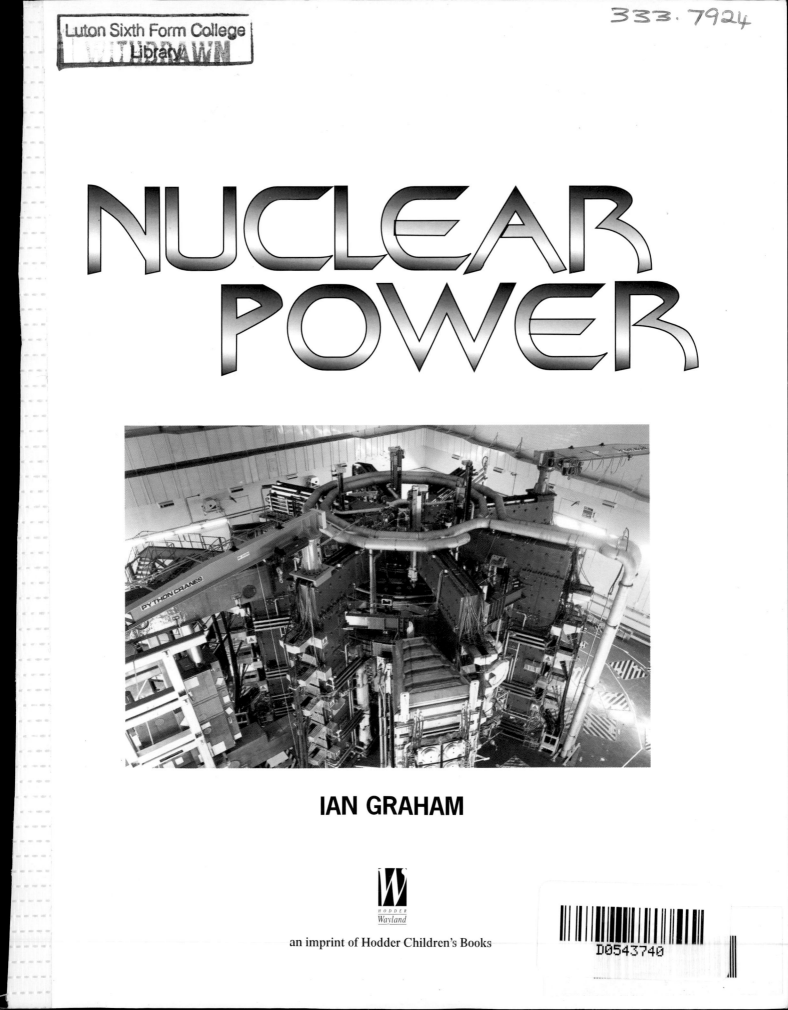

IAN GRAHAM

HODDER
Wayland

an imprint of Hodder Children's Books

ENERGY FOREVER?

Nuclear Power

OTHER TITLES IN THE SERIES

Solar Power · Water Power · Wind Power
Fossil Fuels · Geothermal and Bio-energy

Produced for Hodder Wayland Publishers Ltd by Lionheart Books,
10 Chelmsford Square, London NW10 3AR

Project editor: Lionel Bender
Designer: Ben White
Text editor: Michael March
Picture research: Madeleine Samuel
Electronic make-up: Mike Pilley, Radius/Pelican Graphics
Illustrated by Rudi Vizi

First published in Great Britain in 1998
by Wayland (Publishers) Ltd
Reprinted in 2001 by Hodder Wayland,
an imprint of Hodder Children's Books

© Hodder Wayland 1998

British Library Cataloguing in Publication Data
Graham, Ian, 1953–
Nuclear Power
1.Nuclear power – Juvenile literature
I. Title II. Lionel Bender
571.3

ISBN 0 7502 3327 3

Printed and bound by G.Canale & C.S.p.A., Turin, Italy

All Hodder Wayland books encourage children to read and help them improve their literacy.

✓ The contents page, page numbers, headings and index help to locate a particular piece of information.

✓ The glossary reinforces alphabetic knowledge and extends vocabulary.

✓ The books to read section suggests other books dealing with the same subject.

Picture Acknowledgements
Cover: Ecoscene/Sally Morgan.
AEA Technology, Harwell: 1, 5
top, 8 bottom, 14 right, 17 top,
18 top, 28 top, 29, 31, 33, 37,
41, 44, 45. Biofoto, Denmark:
22 right. British Nuclear Fuels:
6 right, 10, 12, 13, 14 left, 15,
16, 19, 23, 30, 32 (Wayland
Photo Library), 42. Ecoscene:
5 bottom, 11, 27(Close). EDF: 6
left, 34, 35. Ole Steen Hansen:
18 right. Mary Evans Picture
Library: 8 top. Stockmarket: 21,
24, 39. Science Photo Library:
9 (Argonne National
Laboratory), 17 bottom (Martin
Bond), 26 (Novosti), 28 bottom
(Peter Menzel), 36 left (Stevie
Grand), 43 (Sandia National
Laboratories). US Department of
Energy: 22 left, 25, 26 left, 36
right, 40.

CONTENTS

WHAT IS NUCLEAR POWER?

Introduction

Nearly one-fifth of the world's electricity is produced by nuclear power stations. Nuclear power comes from the energy stored inside a nucleus of an atom. Atoms are tiny – much too small to be seen even under the most powerful microscope – but they make up everything in the world around us. The centre of an atom – the nucleus – consists of still smaller particles called protons and neutrons. The number of protons in an atomic nucleus distinguishes the different elements. An atom of hydrogen, the lightest element, has just one proton in the nucleus. An atom of uranium, the heaviest element found in nature, has 92 protons and many more neutrons.

Nuclear fission

Separately, protons and neutrons have more mass – are bigger – than when they are combined in a nucleus. This is because inside the nucleus some of the mass takes the form of 'binding energy', the energy needed to hold the nucleus together. Splitting the nucleus of an atom – a process called nuclear fission – releases the binding energy.

With most elements, nuclear fission is impossible because the nuclei are too tightly bound. However, some elements, such as uranium, are made up of atoms with big, unstable nuclei which are easy to break apart. The energy released – and it is enormous – is the source of nuclear power. This can be used to make electricity, propel a submarine or a ship or, in a weapon, produce a mighty explosion.

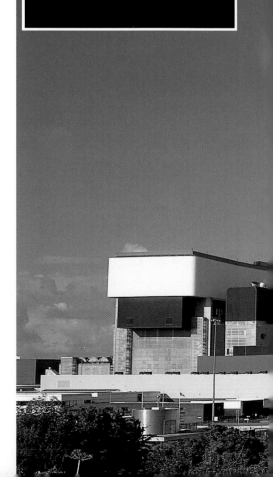

Right: If a slow-moving neutron strikes a uranium atom, the atom's nucleus absorbs the neutron. The nucleus becomes so unstable that it breaks apart. This is called nuclear fission. The result is two large fission products, three neutrons and a burst of energy.

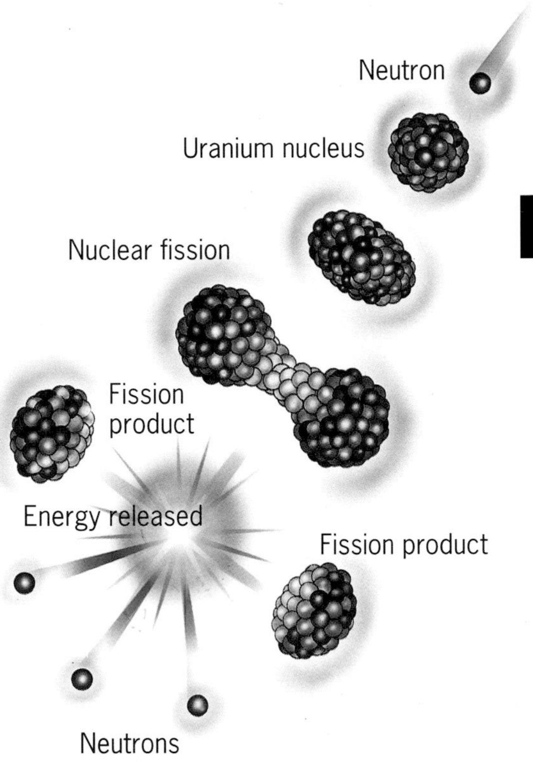

Neutron

Uranium nucleus

Nuclear fission

Fission product

Energy released

Fission product

Neutrons

Nuclear power stations, such as this one at Heysham in England, work round the clock supplying enough electricity to meet the demands of homes, businesses and industry.

When uranium is found near the surface, it is dug out by stripping away the surface soil and rock, forming a vast open pit in the ground. This type of mine is called a strip mine or open-cast mine.

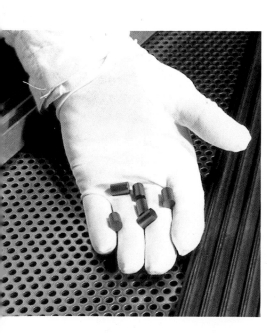

The energy that makes hundreds of megawatts of electricity inside a nuclear power station comes from thousands of these small grey pellets of uranium oxide.

Where do nuclear fuels come from?

The most common nuclear fuel, uranium, is a metal extracted from the Earth's crust. It is the 48th most abundant chemical element. But every particle of uranium found on Earth was once inside a star. Uranium is made when a very big star, called a supernova, explodes and becomes intensely bright. In the heart of the explosion, light nuclei are rammed together to make heavier nuclei, and then scattered across the Universe. Other stars sweep them up and pull them together to make planets.

Uranium ores

Uranium is found in minerals called ores. These are naturally occurring chemical compounds that contain metal, such as uranium, in sufficient quantities as to make extraction worthwhile. The most common uranium ores are pitchblende and carnotite. The richest deposits are found in Canada, the Congo and the USA.

Uranium ores contain three different types, or isotopes, of uranium. Isotopes are elements with the same number of protons in their nuclei, but different numbers of neutrons. Uranium's isotopes are U-238, U-235 and U-234, where 'U' stands for uranium. More than 99 per cent of the uranium found in nature is U-238, but U-235 is the only naturally occurring uranium isotope that will easily undergo nuclear fission.

Most of Africa is non-nuclear because of the high cost of nuclear technology. Australia has large uranium deposits, but is a non-nuclear continent. Most of its energy is supplied by coal-fired power stations and hydroelectric schemes.

☐ Nuclear power

● Uranium mining

Marja Sklodowska, better known as Marie Curie, her married name, discovered two new radioactive elements – radium and polonium. In 1911, she was awarded the Nobel Prize for Chemistry in recognition of her pioneering research.

How long has nuclear power been used?

Radioactivity was discovered by the scientist Henri Becquerel in 1896. He noticed that photographic plates inside lightproof packs had darkened as if they had been exposed to light. The dark patch on the film was in the same place as a piece of rock, containing uranium, that had been sitting on top of the plates. The uranium had given out radiation in the form of invisible particles and it was these that produced the dark patch. Two years later, the Polish-born French scientist Marie Curie invented the word 'radioactive' to describe materials that behaved like this. She and her husband Pierre found that a mineral called pitchblende was also radioactive. This turned out to be a previously unknown element, which she called radium.

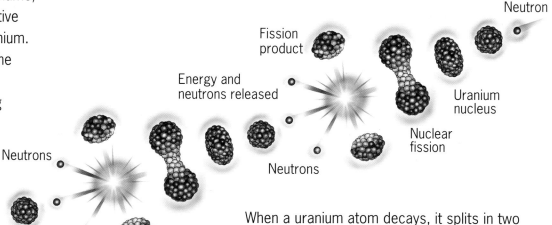

When a uranium atom decays, it splits in two and sends out three neutrons. If one of these neutrons hits another uranium atom and makes that decay too, more neutrons are flung out to make more uranium atoms decay and so on. The chain reaction keeps going and releases a steady flow of energy.

To make electricity, uranium must release energy steadily over a long period of time. This continuing process is called a chain reaction. This painting shows the first controlled and sustained nuclear chain reaction, achieved by the Italian physicist Enrico Fermi working at the University of Chicago, USA, in December 1942.

Nuclear science

Before radioactivity was discovered, scientists thought that atoms were the smallest particles of matter. But the discovery of alpha and beta particles flying out of radioactive materials showed this to be wrong. Alpha particles are nuclei consisting of two protons and two neutrons. Beta particles are much smaller particles ejected from nuclei. Disintegration of the nuclei causes one element to change into another. This process is called radioactive decay. Its discovery resulted in a new branch of scientific research, leading to nuclear power stations and nuclear weapons.

FACTFILE

The first peaceful, practical use of nuclear power was in 1951, when an experimental nuclear reactor in Idaho Falls, USA, became the first to generate electricity. A reactor in Obninsk, in Russia, produced 100 megawatts of electricity in 1955. The world's first commercial nuclear power station went into service at Calder Hall in Cumbria, UK, in 1956. The first US prototype nuclear power station began operating in 1957.

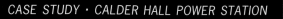

Uranium is the most commonly used nuclear fuel. A tonne of uranium produces the same amount of energy as 25,000 tonnes of coal or 100,000 barrels (15.9m litres) of oil.

The Calder Hall nuclear power station in West Cumbria, England, has been operating for more than 40 years. It has four reactors housed inside steel pressure cylinders. Each reactor contains 10,000 natural uranium fuel elements.

Magnox reactors

Calder Hall, the first nuclear power station, is in the northwest of England. It uses a type of nuclear reactor called a Magnox reactor. The fuel is natural uranium, containing mostly U-238 and only 0.7 per cent U-235. It is in the form of rods, called fuel elements, encased in tubes of Magnox, a magnesium alloy.

Neutrons from radioactive decay in the fuel are slowed down by graphite blocks between the fuel elements. Slowing down the neutrons makes them more likely to be absorbed by the U-235 in the fuel, causing more fissions and so releasing more energy in the form of heat.

Controlling power levels

The rate of fissions and therefore the amount of heat produced by the reactor can be adjusted by raising or lowering control rods between the fuel elements. The control rods absorb neutrons and stop them from splitting any more atoms in the fuel. Energy is carried away from the reactor by a coolant, which absorbs heat from the fuel.

In the Magnox reactor, carbon dioxide gas is the coolant. It passes through the reactor to become hot, and then transfers this heat to water. The water boils and makes steam, which then drives a turbogenerator, a turbine linked to an electricity generator.

Calder Hall is located at the site better known as Sellafield. Magnox reactors are only about 25 per cent efficient, compared to 35 per cent efficiency for coal-fired power stations.

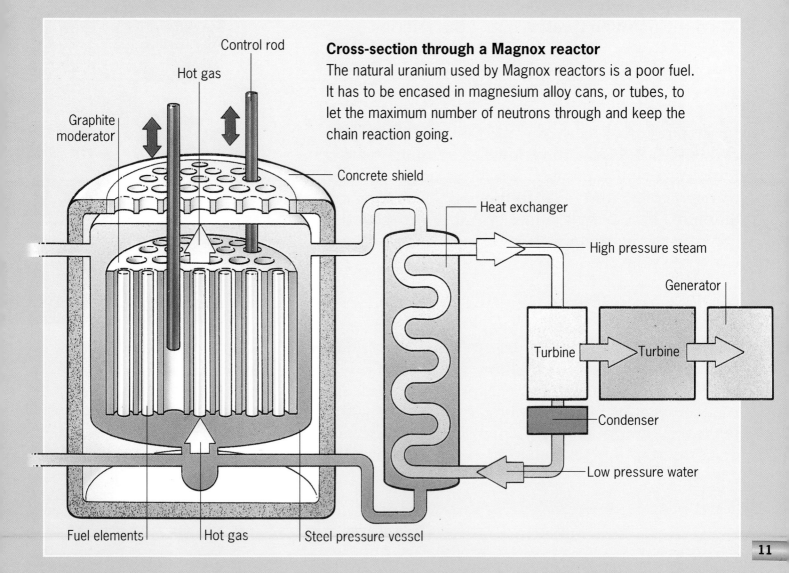

Cross-section through a Magnox reactor
The natural uranium used by Magnox reactors is a poor fuel. It has to be encased in magnesium alloy cans, or tubes, to let the maximum number of neutrons through and keep the chain reaction going.

Control rod

Hot gas

Graphite moderator

Concrete shield

Heat exchanger

High pressure steam

Generator

Turbine

Turbine

Condenser

Low pressure water

Fuel elements

Hot gas

Steel pressure vessel

Making nuclear fuels

About 30,000 tonnes of uranium is mined every year. Uranium ore dug out of the ground cannot be used in nuclear power stations, because there is too little uranium in it – about 2 per cent or less. The ore has to be processed to extract the uranium.

First the ore is crushed and dissolved in acid to separate the uranium metal from the unwanted rock material. Then the uranium is taken out of the solution as uranium oxide, which is known as yellowcake. This is transported to conversion plants where it is changed into uranium dioxide reactor fuel.

In an alternative method, called solvent extraction, two bore-holes are drilled down to uranium-bearing rock. A solvent is pumped down one hole. It passes through cracks and holes in the rock, dissolving out the uranium. The solvent comes up out of the second hole, carrying the uranium with it. The uranium is then extracted from the solvent.

Plutonium

Some reactors and also nuclear weapons use a different type of nuclear fuel called plutonium. Only a tiny amount of plutonium exists in nature. Most of it is made inside nuclear reactors by bombarding uranium-238 with neutrons. Plutonium is extremely dangerous because it gives out high-energy radiation and it is particularly explosive.

Work is completed on a batch of fuel cans destined for a Magnox reactor. Fins on the cans greatly increase their surface area so that they give up heat to the coolant flowing through the reactor more efficiently.

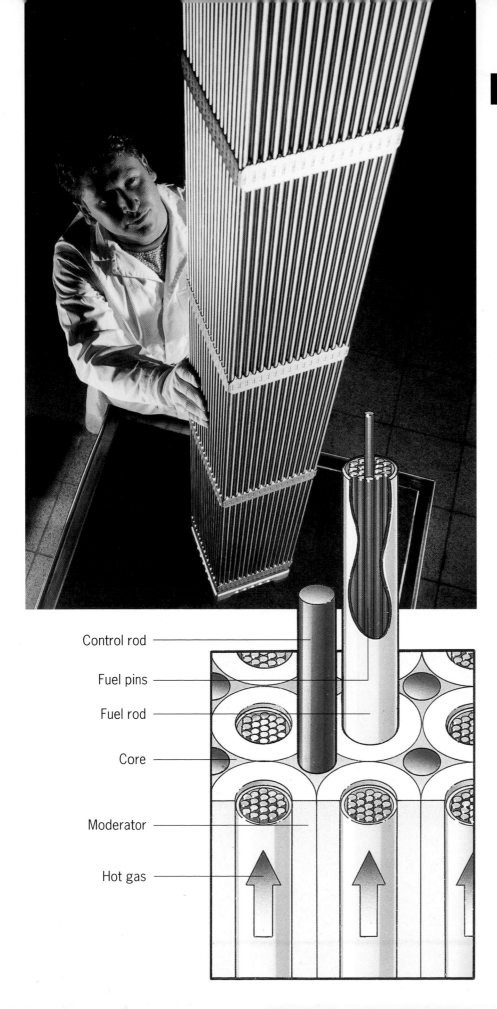

Plutonium is used as a source of energy for devices that have to be small and lightweight and have to work reliably for years at a time. Some early heart pacemakers, which keep a damaged or diseased heart beating normally, were powered by plutonium. Deep space probes, including the Cassini-Huygens spacecraft that is on its way to Saturn, have plutonium-powered electricity generators.

A fuel assembly for a PWR (pressurized water reactor) receives its final inspection. Each assembly contains 298 uranium fuel pins.

Control rod

Fuel pins

Fuel rod

Core

Moderator

Hot gas

Fuel rods are packed inside tubes, or cans, which are embedded in a moderator. The moderator can be graphite, light (ordinary) water or heavy water. Its job is to slow down neutrons so that they are more likely to be absorbed by the fuel atoms and cause fissions. Control rods made from a material such as boron, which absorbs neutrons, can be lowered into the core to slow down the chain reaction.

Reprocessing spent fuel

As a nuclear power station's fuel decays, it produces less and less heat energy and eventually has to be replaced with new fuel. The old fuel can be 'reprocessed' to extract uranium that has not yet decayed, so that it can be used again.

It is worth reprocessing nuclear fuel because one tonne of reprocessed fuel provides the same amount of energy as 20,000 tonnes of oil. Most of the world's nuclear fuel reprocessing is carried out in France, the UK, Japan and Germany. Other countries transport their nuclear fuel to these countries for treatment.

Above: Spent fuel rods glow in the storage pond at Britain's Atomic Energy Research Establishment (AERE), Harwell. The blue glow, called Cerenkov radiation, is not heat. It is caused when particles travel faster through a material than the speed of light in that material.

Left: Spent fuel from nuclear power stations cools in a storage pond at Britain's Thermal Oxide Reprocessing Plant (THORP). Spent fuel gives out a lot of heat. It has to be cooled for up to 50 years before it can be reprocessed and disposed of.

When spent fuel is cool enough for reprocessing to start, the first job is to strip off the metal fuel cans and get the fuel out. Here, Magnox fuel rods are being decanned before reprocessing.

Nuclear waste

As well as providing fuel for reprocessing, nuclear power stations also produce their own waste. Waste is divided into three groups – low-level, intermediate-level and high-level – depending on how radioactive it is. It can be solid, liquid or gas.

Low-level waste includes workers' clothing, air filters and old equipment that has been contaminated very little by radioactivity. Intermediate-level waste includes used fuel cans and chemicals from waste-treatment processes. High-level waste consists mostly of liquid chemicals. Each type of radioactive waste is handled and stored differently.

Reprocessing on a global scale

Nuclear fuel has been reprocessed in France since 1958. The COGEMA reprocessing plant, situated at Cap de la Hague on the tip of the Cotentin peninsula in France, has reprocessed nuclear fuel since 1966. It is now the world's largest LWR (light water reactor) reprocessing plant. It reprocesses fuel for France and 27 other countries using nuclear electricity (mainly Belgium, Germany, Japan, the Netherlands and Switzerland). It can reprocess up to 680 tonnes of spent fuel per year. More than 10,000 tonnes of fuel for light water reactors have been reprocessed at La Hague since it opened.

The COGEMA nuclear reprocessing plant stretches across the countryside on France's Channel coast near Cherbourg.

Underwater storage

Fuel assemblies arriving at the plant are placed in baskets and stored underwater for several years until they have cooled down and become less radioactive. The fuel rods are then cut into 3-centimetre lengths, dissolved in acid and separated into uranium, plutonium and waste products. The uranium and plutonium are used to make new fuel.

Fresh, reprocessed uranium can be handled with ease and safety. Here, fuel pins have been inserted into a fuel element for an AGR (advanced gas-cooled reactor).

Below: A view of the COGEMA plant at night. Radioactive waste from the reprocessing is stored locally.

A scientist takes grass samples to check radiation levels in the environment around the Hunterston B nuclear power station near Largs on the coast of Scotland.

Environmental impact

Nuclear power stations do not cause air pollution, as happens when power is generated by burning coal or gas. But some of the waste materials that they do produce remain dangerously radioactive for thousands of years to come. Nuclear fuel is so dangerous that it must never be allowed to escape into the environment.

Workers in the nuclear industry wear dosimeters which record how much, if any, radiation they have been exposed to. The air inside nuclear power stations is constantly monitored so that any leaks of radioactive gas are detected immediately. Some countries, such as Sweden, have decided not to build any more nuclear power stations because nuclear power is considered too much of a hazard. Other countries, including France and Japan, are continuing to develop their nuclear power industries.

ATOMKRAFT? NEJ TAK

Nuclear Power? No Thanks! – a badge worn by people in Denmark in the late 1970s. Massive popular protest in forced the Danish government to abandon the idea of building nuclear power stations in Denmark.

Nuclear dumping

In the past, waste from civilian and military nuclear reactors in some countries was simply dumped in the sea or in deep lakes, or buried in the ground. Because of this, parts of the former Soviet Union are so contaminated that a visitor could receive a lethal dose of radiation just by standing beside a lake where radioactive waste was dumped. Nuclear leaks and dumped waste from past decades continue to affect us today and will affect future generations too.

A nuclear worker checks his radiation monitors before entering a radioactive area. Monitors are worn all the time in these areas and checked regularly to ensure that workers are not exposed to dangerous levels of radiation.

FACTFILE

Radioactivity is measured in Becquerels. A Becquerel (symbol Bq) is one radioactive disintegration, or decay, per second. A radiation level of 37,000 million decays per second is also known as a curie (Ci), named after Marie Curie. Radiation absorbed by the human body is measured in grays. One gray (Gy) is equivalent to 1joule of energy per kg of body weight.

Biological effects of radiation

High doses of radiation destroy life. The first use of nuclear power was the devastating attack on the Japanese city of Hiroshima in 1945. This, together with a second attack on Nagasaki, a Japanese port, brought World War II to an abrupt end. Most of Hiroshima was flattened and about 100,000 people were killed by the one bomb. The bomb dropped on Nagasaki destroyed a third of the city and killed 66,000 people. The radiation that was spread over these cities by the bombs has continued to affect people until the present day.

Radioactive materials produce three types of radiation – alpha, beta and gamma. Alpha and beta radiation are particles. Gamma radiation is an electromagnetic wave like light but more penetrating. Alpha particles can be stopped by a sheet of paper. Beta radiation is made up of much smaller particles called electrons. They can be stopped by a thin sheet of aluminium. To stop gamma radiation a thick wall of concrete or lead is needed.

Exposure to radiation

Iodine-13, a radioactive isotope of iodine, collects in the thyroid gland.

The muscles absorb caesium-134 and caesium-137.

Carbon-14, a radioactive isotope of carbon, is taken in with food into the liver or stomach.

Strontium-90 is absorbed by the bones and can cause bone cancer or leukaemia.

Radiation can damage or kill living cells by breaking the DNA molecule inside the cell's nucleus. DNA contains the code that controls the day-to-day functioning of the cells as well as the production of new cells.

Penetrative power of radiation

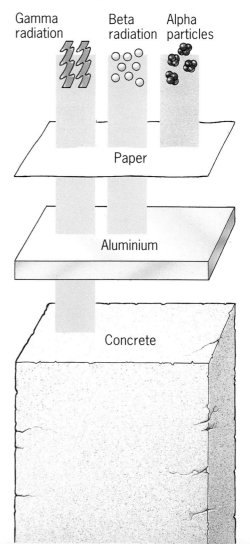

Gamma radiation   Beta radiation   Alpha particles

Paper

Aluminium

Concrete

A nuclear explosion produces the tell-tale mushroom-shaped cloud. The explosive force of the detonation can destroy an entire city in seconds. Even people who survive the blast may suffer for the rest of their lives from the radiation produced by the bomb.

FACTFILE

Luminous watch dials used to be made by hand. The people who painted the luminous spots on the dials often licked their brushes into a fine point. The paint they used was radioactive. Some of these workers later developed mouth cancers as a result.

Radiation sickness

Even a low dose of radiation can make people feel ill. Higher doses cause ulcers and burns on the skin and damage the bone marrow, where red blood cells are made. This reduces the body's ability to fight off infections. Breathing in radioactive particles damages the lungs. In the longer term, over a number of years or decades, nuclear radiation causes cancers. Radiation can even harm people who are not yet born. It can damage DNA in the cells of the living, so that faulty instructions for growth and development are passed on to their unborn children.

Transporting nuclear fuels

Nuclear fuel has to be taken from where it is processed to the reactors where it is used. Spent fuel – uranium and other materials that have reached the end of their useful life as reactor fuel – must be transported from power stations for reprocessing and storage. Nuclear materials are carried by specially designed ships and railway wagons.

In the USA, spent fuel from nuclear power stations is transported inside enormously strong casks on railroad flatcars. Each of these specially designed casks is 7.1 metres long, 3 metres in diameter and weighs 80–90 tonnes when fully loaded.

Spent fuel and reactor core materials from Swedish nuclear power stations are transported by this ship, *Sigyn*, to Britain or France for reprocessing or storage.

Flasks containing spent fuel from British nuclear power stations are transported by rail to the reprocessing plant at Sellafield in Cumbria. The design and construction of flasks used to transport nuclear fuel are strictly controlled by international agreements.

Nuclear flasks

Nuclear fuel must not be allowed to leak or escape while it is being moved, even if the ship or train transporting it were to be involved in a serious accident. The fuel is carried inside special containers called flasks. They are designed to seal the radiation inside and withstand any accident or even a deliberate attack by terrorists. Each flask is made from steel, weighs between 50 and 110 tonnes and can cost up to £1,000,000. It is built to survive being dropped from a height of 9 metres onto a flat hard surface and from 1 metre onto a sharp point. And it must be able to survive a fire at 800°C for half an hour.

FACTFILE

One nuclear flask was tested for strength in the UK by crashing a diesel locomotive and three carriages into it at 160km/h. When the dust settled, the locomotive had been completely destroyed but the flask survived and did not leak.

Storing nuclear waste

Because they are radioactive, the waste products from nuclear power stations need to be disposed of very carefully. Burning would release them into the atmosphere. Burying them in a normal waste dump would allow the radiation to escape into the ground and contaminate water supplies. Different storage methods are used for nuclear waste depending on the level of radioactivity. Most low- and intermediate-level waste is sealed in containers and stored above ground at special sites. Later it may be stored underground. High-level waste is often set hard in glass bricks (a process called vitrification) before being buried deep underground. But the ground must be absolutely stable, with no danger of earthquake or volcano.

FACTFILE

Not everything nuclear is dangerous. Natural uranium can be handled safely because it decays so slowly that it does no harm.

At Hanford nuclear waste storage facility in the US, spent plutonium fuel is kept underground in huge waste tanks.

Burial at sea

Currently, nuclear waste burial sites are all on land. An alternative option is to bury the waste deep underneath the seabed. There are parts of the sea floor that have been stable for millions of years. Scientists believe that the fine ocean sediments would seal any leaks in the waste containers and stop radiation from spreading. In about 1,000 years, the metal waste containers would have corroded, allowing the radioactive waste to reach the surrounding mud. But scientists say that it would spread only 1 metre in 24,000 years.

At a US plutonium and uranium recovery and waste processing plant, a technician uses a robotic arm and safety cabinet to handle radioactive waste material ready for storage.

Solid waste is prepared for burial by first encasing it in concrete inside drums. The drums are then packed into tanks, which are loaded into underground vaults, and the vaults are filled with concrete. Each stage is designed to provide another barrier to stop the radiation from leaking out into the surrounding ground.

Drum filled with solid waste

Drums in storage units

Storage units in tunnel

Tunnel filled in and sealed

Rock layers

Tunnels in seabed

Sea

Below: This computer simulation shows how far radioactive material blasted into the atmosphere by the accident at Chernobyl had spread around the world only 10 days after the explosion.

Right: An aerial view of the damaged reactor at Chernobyl. People living closest to Chernobyl received the highest radiation doses and have suffered from serious health problems as a result. Nine million people all over Europe and Scandinavia were affected by the accident in one way or another.

A major disaster

Designers of nuclear power stations try to predict what might go wrong, how it might go wrong and how any accident or fault can best be detected and handled without allowing any radiation to escape. There have been nuclear accidents in the USA and the UK, but the world's worst nuclear accident so far occurred on 26 April 1986 at Chernobyl, about 130 kilometres north of Kiev in the Ukraine. One of the four reactors at the Chernobyl nuclear power station exploded and caught fire, spreading radioactive dust and gas over a huge area.

What went wrong?

While a test was being carried out on the reactor, its power output began to rise. Operators could not lower the control rods quickly enough to stop the fuel from overheating. Coolant water inside the reactor flashed to steam. The steam reacted with graphite in the reactor and exploded. With water and hot fuel now mixing together inside the reactor, there were more explosions, which started fires. The explosions were powerful enough to lift off the reactor's 1,000-tonne lid and scatter highly radioactive fuel all around. Heavy particles fell nearby, but small particles were carried away by the wind, with devastating results.

FACTFILE

Fires in the Chernobyl 4 reactor carried tiny radioactive particles high into the air where they could be carried hundreds of kilometres by the wind. A radioactive cloud spread westwards across northern Europe and Scandinavia. It was detected in Sweden two days after the accident.

Some British sheep were contaminated by radioactive fallout from Chernobyl. It settled on the sheep and also on the grass that they ate. The sheep were tested for radiation levels and contaminated sheep were marked with a coloured dye.

Power stations

There are about 420 nuclear power stations in the world today. About a quarter of them are in the USA. Power stations are giant steam engines. They use heat supplied by a fuel to boil water and make steam, which drives a turbogenerator to make electricity. The only difference between nuclear power stations and other power stations is the type of fuel they use and the way the fuel gives up its heat. Fossil fuels – coal and gas – have to be burned to release the energy stored inside them, while nuclear fuel gives out heat without burning.

Dozens of instruments in a nuclear power station's control room enable people to monitor and control everything that is happening in the reactor, turbines and generating hall.

Steam rises from the cooling towers at Rancho Seco nuclear power station in California, USA. Nuclear reactors produce heat, which is transferred to water to make steam. The steam turns the shaft of a turbine. The spinning shaft transfers its energy to a generator, which converts the movement into electrical energy.

Pipes carry steam into turbines behind the generators in the generator hall at a nuclear power station.

Nuclear reactors

There are two types of nuclear reactors – thermal reactors and fast reactors. The majority of nuclear power stations have thermal reactors. The chain reaction is kept going by slow-moving neutrons, which are also called thermal neutrons.

In fast reactors, the fissions are produced by fast neutrons as, unlike thermal reactors, fast reactors have no moderator to slow the neutrons down. That is why they are known as fast reactors. Without the need for a moderator, fast reactors can be made considerably smaller in size than thermal reactors. They also use a different fuel – a mixture of plutonium and uranium.

Thermal reactors

There are many different designs of thermal reactors in service in different parts of the world. Most of them are known by a set of initials for words that describe how they work. Magnox, AGR (Advanced Gas-cooled Reactor), PWR (Pressurized Water Reactor), BWR (Boiling Water Reactor), CANDU (CANadian Deuterium Uranium), SGHWR (Steam Generating Heavy Water Reactor), HTR (High Temperature Reactor) and the Russian RBMK (Russian Graphite Moderated Channel Tube, in Russian) are all types of thermal reactors.

Grühnde power station in Germany is a PWR (Pressurized Water Reactor), the most popular type of reactor today. The dome-shaped building just left of centre is the reactor room.

The PWR was developed in the USA and the former Soviet Union as a power plant for ships and submarines. It is now the world's most widely used type of nuclear reactor for making electricity. It uses ordinary water under great pressure as both a coolant and a moderator (to slow down the neutrons). Reactors that use ordinary water in this way are also known as light water reactors.

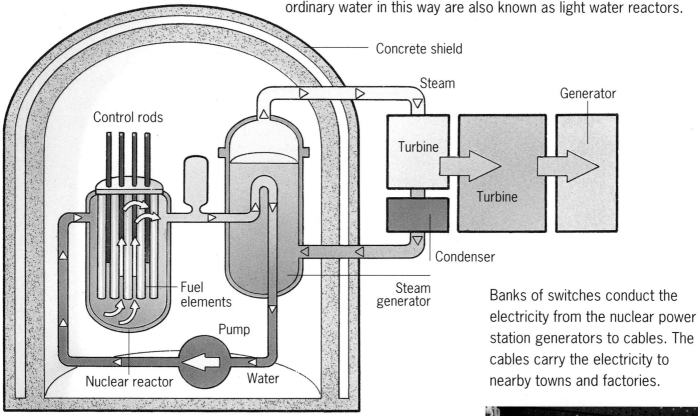

Thermal reactor fuel

Thermal reactors differ from each other in the coolant and fuel they use. Some use a gas to carry heat away from the reactor, Others use a liquid coolant. And while all thermal reactors use uranium fuel, the amounts of U-235 and U-238 in the fuel differ in each type.

Most thermal reactors use enriched uranium fuel. This is uranium that has been processed so that it contains more U-235 than is found in natural uranium. Boosting the amount of U-235 increases the chances of nuclear fissions occurring. A higher fission rate produces more heat, which increases the reactor's power output. Only Magnox and CANDU reactors use natural, rather than enriched, uranium.

Banks of switches conduct the electricity from the nuclear power station generators to cables. The cables carry the electricity to nearby towns and factories.

Fast reactors

Fast reactors use uranium more efficiently than thermal reactors. Thermal reactors convert about one-third of the heat energy from the fuel into electricity. Fast reactors convert about half of the heat into electricity. Uranium waste from thermal reactors can be used as fuel in fast reactors, which use a mixture of uranium and plutonium as fuel. About one-fifth of the fuel is plutonium.

Plutonium undergoes fission easily and keeps the chain reaction going, so no moderator is needed. Fast reactors are small and produce a lot of heat. Liquid sodium is used as a coolant because it carries heat away efficiently. The main disadvantage of using liquid sodium is that it bursts into flames if it comes into contact with water!

Making more fuel

The core of a fast reactor can be surrounded with a 'blanket' of uranium-238. When this is bombarded by neutrons, it is gradually transformed into plutonium. So, fast reactors are also called fast breeder reactors because they produce, or breed, more fuel than they use.

The UK's prototype fast reactor is housed inside the white dome at Dounreay on the coast of Scotland. Designed to produce 250 megawatts of electricity, it has been working since 1975.

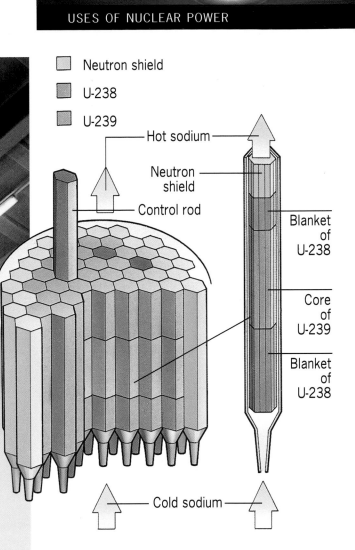

Neutron shield

U-238

U-239

Hot sodium

Neutron shield

Control rod

Blanket of U-238

Core of U-239

Blanket of U-238

Cold sodium

Heat from fuel in the compact reactor core heats up the liquid sodium coolant. This is pumped through a heat exchanger, where it heats a second coolant, also liquid sodium. The second coolant heats water to produce steam, which powers a turbogenerator.

At Dounreay, a fuel assembly is moved to the reactor. It is lowered by crane into position in the top of the reactor.

The Superphénix reactor core is located in the tall building in the background of this photo. It is cooled by about 5,000 tonnes of liquid sodium. In order to shut the reactor down, this liquid sodium coolant will have to be removed. It will be drained gradually as the fuel is removed.

Below: Pellets of uranium and plutonium fuel were piled up in steel tubes inside the core of the French fast breeder reactor Superphénix. More than 10,000 pellets were used.

From production to research

France's first fast breeder reactor was called Superphénix. It was built at Creys-Malville, near Lyon, in the 1970s. Construction started in December 1974 and the reactor started operating on 9 December1986. It produced 1,240 megawatts of electricity.

Superphénix was built as a commercial reactor to produce electricity. All nuclear reactors are licensed and controlled by national and international regulations, to ensure that they operate as safely as possible. In 1994, the licence for Superphénix was changed. It was to cease being a power reactor, generating electricity, and become a reactor used for scientific research.

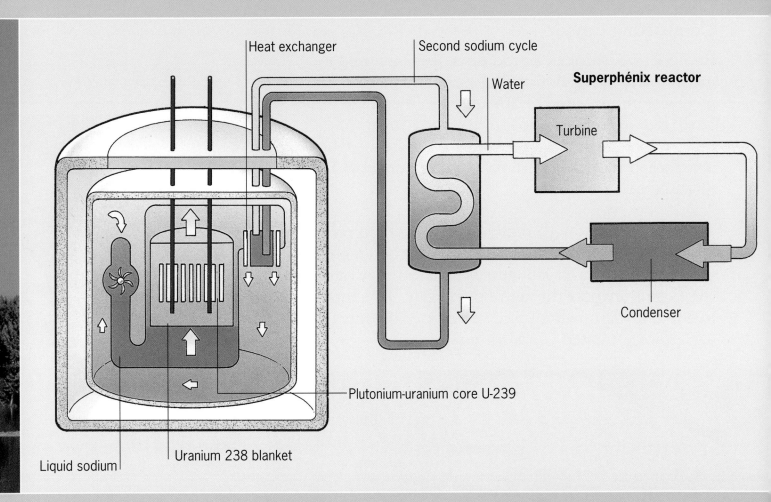

Heat exchanger

Second sodium cycle

Water

Superphénix reactor

Turbine

Condenser

Plutonium-uranium core U-239

Uranium 238 blanket

Liquid sodium

The new licence for Superphénix was cancelled in February 1997. And on 19 June 1997, France's newly elected Prime Minister, Lionel Jospin, announced that Superphénix would be shut down permanently for reasons of cost.

Shutting down a nuclear reactor permanently and dismantling it is called decommissioning. Superphénix operated for the last time in December 1996, 10 years after it entered service.

The Superphénix reactor is housed inside a containment vessel. Three layers – the inner tank, main reactor vessel and outer safety vessel – are designed to stop any radioactive material from escaping. The whole reactor is contained inside a thick concrete shield.

Combatting cancer

Radioactive isotopes, or radioisotopes, are used in medicine to treat serious illnesses. Cobalt-60 is the most commonly used radioisotope in medicine today. Early research into radioactivity had shown that radioactive materials could burn the skin. In 1904 it was shown that radioactivity from radium could kill diseased cells.

Treating patients with radiation is called radiotherapy. Beams of radiation from radioisotopes can reach deep inside the body and kill cancer cells without harming the flesh they pass through on the way. Tumours deep inside the brain, which once could not be operated on, can now be treated by radiotherapy.

Above: A row of devices called calutrons at the US Oak Ridge National Laboratory produces radioisotopes for use all over the world in medicine, industry, research and farming.

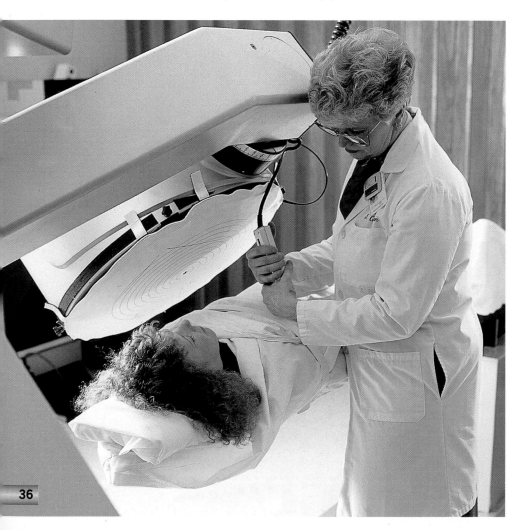

A woman receives a gamma scan of her chest to detect the distribution of a radioactive marker. Gamma scans are used to detect and keep under control cancers in the body.

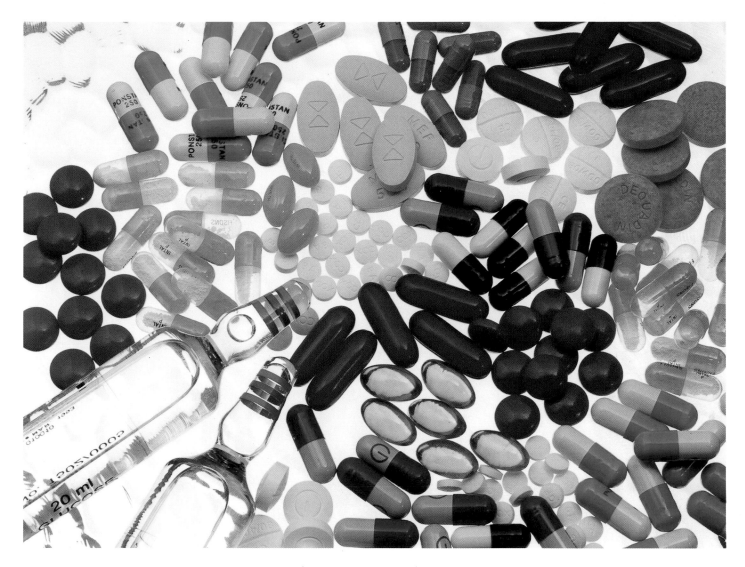

Radioactive markers travel around the body. The markers may be injected into the bloodstream, or taken in tablets or capsules, which are swallowed. The amount of a marker that is absorbed by an organ shows how well the organ is working.

Radioactive markers

Weakly radioactive materials injected into one part of the body can be tracked as they are carried to other parts of the body. By attaching the radioactive material to a food or drug, it is possible to study the way the food or drug is absorbed by the body and where it ends up.

Iodine-131 is taken up by the thyroid gland, offering a way of measuring how active this gland is. Other isotopes are taken up from the blood by the brain, providing a way of measuring activity in different parts of the brain.

Nuclear-powered vehicles

Small lightweight nuclear reactors can power vehicles, especially ships, submarines and spacecraft. Because of the cost of developing nuclear technology, the difficulties of operating it and the hazards of working with radiation, the majority of nuclear-powered vehicles are military.

Powering submarines by nuclear reactors enables them to stay submerged for up to several months at a time, hidden underwater and able to roam the world's oceans unseen. The first civilian nuclear-powered ship, the *Savannah*, a 22,000-tonne cargo ship, was built in the USA in 1962. And nuclear powered ice-breaking ships were built in Russia. However, the expense and the dangers of nuclear power have prevented nuclear-powered vehicles from becoming more popular.

FACTFILE

The first nuclear-powered submarine was the US Navy's Nautilus. It was launched in 1954 and immediately broke all the previous submarine records for speed and time spent submerged. In 1958 it became the first submarine to travel from the Atlantic Ocean to the Pacific underneath the north polar ice cap. Nuclear power enabled it to travel 2,945 kilometres underwater.

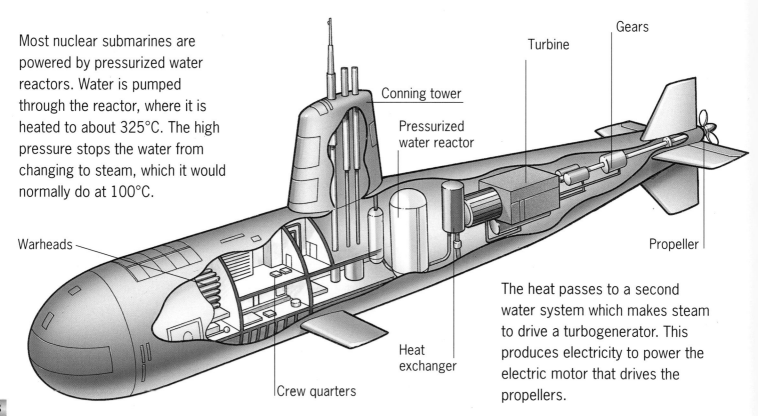

Most nuclear submarines are powered by pressurized water reactors. Water is pumped through the reactor, where it is heated to about 325°C. The high pressure stops the water from changing to steam, which it would normally do at 100°C.

Warheads

Crew quarters

Conning tower

Pressurized water reactor

Heat exchanger

Turbine

Gears

Propeller

The heat passes to a second water system which makes steam to drive a turbogenerator. This produces electricity to power the electric motor that drives the propellers.

Nuclear submarines can stay underwater much longer than diesel-powered submarines. Nuclear engines do not 'burn' their fuel, so they can work without producing fumes or using up precious oxygen.

Nuclear-powered spacecraft

Most spacecraft instruments, radios and cameras are powered by electricity produced from sunlight by solar panels. The farther a spacecraft travels from the Sun, the less sunlight there is for making electricity. Beyond the orbit of Mars, there is not enough light to use solar panels. Instead, space probes sent to study the solar system's outer planets – Jupiter, Saturn, Uranus, Neptune and Pluto – as well as asteroids and comets, are powered by tiny nuclear reactors.

A nuclear weapon is a complicated device. This American B-61 nuclear bomb has no fewer than 6,000 parts.

Nuclear weapons

The discovery that small amounts of matter could be converted into huge amounts of energy was of great interest to military forces. One kilogram of matter changed completely into energy would produce as much energy as exploding 22 million tonnes of normal explosives. The first nuclear bombs were fission weapons. They worked by ramming enough plutonium together so that the rate of fissions soared and released an immense burst of energy, the explosion. Hydrogen bombs followed. They worked by ramming different hydrogen isotopes together to produce an even more powerful explosion.

Below: A nuclear missile is a rocket with a nuclear bomb on top. The largest missiles have up to three stages, each one a separate rocket in itself. As each stage uses up its fuel, it falls away to save weight. The final stage carries the nuclear payload, or warhead, to its target. Some nuclear missiles are designed to explode when they hit their target. Others are designed to explode in the air above the target.

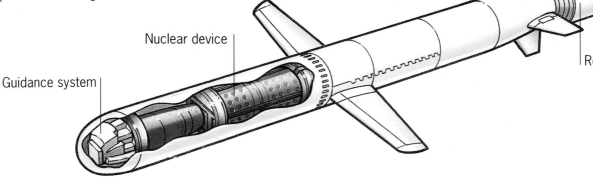

Guidance system

Nuclear device

Rocket booster

Triggering explosions

The minimum amount of material needed to cause a runaway chain reaction and explosion is called the critical mass. In a fission weapon, ordinary explosives are used to ram pieces of plutonium together to form a critical mass that will explode. A hydrogen bomb is a fusion weapon. It explosive power comes from the energy released by joining – or fusing – the nuclei of light elements, rather than splitting the nuclei of heavy ones. But a hydrogen bomb needs a fission bomb to trigger it, as this is the only way to create the high temperatures needed for fusion to take place.

FACTFILE

Submarines armed with nuclear missiles patrol the world's oceans. Nuclear weapons have only ever been used twice. They were the bombs dropped by US aircraft on Japan in 1945. At that time, the USA was the only country with nuclear weapons. Since then, nine more countries have developed their own nuclear weapons.

In the safety of an enclosed cabinet at Dounreay faster breeder reactor site in the UK, a technician studies plutonium waste. Irradiated fuel from the reactor is separated into plutonium, uranium and waste materials. Some of the plutonium is used to make nuclear weapons.

THE FUTURE OF NUCLEAR POWER

FACTFILE

Fusing only 15 grammes of tritium and 10 grammes of deuterium would produce a lifetime's electricity for one person. Hydrogen and deuterium are found in seawater. The deuterium in 1 litre of seawater produces as much energy as burning 300 litres of petrol.

If all our electricity were from nuclear power, the radioactive waste produced in generating the electricity used by one person during their lifetime could be contained in a glass block the size of the palm of your hand.

Nuclear fusion

In the next century, nuclear power stations may work in a different way, using safer fuel that is not radioactive and does not produce radioactive waste. That fuel is hydrogen.

If hydrogen nuclei are slammed together with enough force, they combine to become helium nuclei and produce a burst of energy. This is the principle behind the hydrogen bomb. But there the fusion reaction and the energy released are uncontrolled. The challenge is to design a reactor where the energy from nuclear fusion can be harnessed to produce electricity.

Star power

Nuclear fusion requires temperatures of millions of degrees to make the nuclei move fast enough and collide with enough force to make them fuse together. The only place in nature where nuclear fusion occurs is at the centre of stars. So scientists have been trying to build a nuclear reactor that works like the centre of the Sun. In fact, they have already done it, but the reactor will only work for a few seconds at a time.

To make electricity, the experimental reactor will have to work reliably and controllably for decades. Fusion reactors use rare isotopes of hydrogen, called deuterium and tritium. Deuterium comes from water, and tritium can be made from lithium, a light metal found in rock and mineral springs. Both deuterium and tritium are heavier than normal hydrogen and fuse more easily.

At Sandia National Laboratories in the USA, electricity flashes over the surface of water covering the Particle Beam Fusion Accelerator. A beam of atomic particles is fired a pellet of deuterium and tritium, causing a nuclear fusion reaction. This lasts only a split-second, but creates more than five million million watts.

The Joint European Torus (JET) is a massive structure. The red, eight-legged transformer that surrounds the reactor core and generates the powerful magnetic fields needed to contain the fuel inside it weighs 2,700 tonnes.

FACTFILE

Fusion reactors like JET are also called tokamaks. Tokamak is a word made from parts of the Russian words meaning toroidal (doughnut-shaped) magnetic chamber. The tokamak was invented by the Russian physicist Lev Andreevitch Artsimovitch and first used in 1963.

Handling hot fuel

The Joint European Torus (JET) is an experimental nuclear fusion reactor located at the Culham Laboratory near Oxford, England. It cost $500 million to build, which was paid for by the countries of the European Union. It started operating in 1983.

JET's deuterium and tritium fuel is held in place by two magnetic fields. One is produced by 32 D-shaped electromagnets. The other is produced by an enormous electric current of up to 7 million amps flowing through the fuel itself. This electric current heats the fuel. Radio waves provide extra heating. The fuel is heated to over 100 million°C. At such an incredibly high temperature, electrons are stripped away from atoms, leaving just nuclei. This super-hot state of matter is called a plasma. The nuclei crash into each other and fuse together. An enormous amount of energy is needed to create and contain the plasma. The challenge for JET's designers is to persuade the reactor to produce more energy than it consumes.

Looking down on the top of START, the Small Tight Aspect Ratio Tokomak, at Culham Science Centre in the UK. SMART is an experimental fusion device.

Magnets

JET's reactor core is a metal doughnut 6m across and 4.2m high. It weighs 100 tonnes. Before the deuterium and tritium fuel is allowed in, all the air is pumped out of the core.

Shielding

Vacuum reactor vessel

Reactor core

GLOSSARY

Advanced gas-cooled reactor
One type of thermal reactor.

Alpha particle
A particle flung out by a decaying atom. It contains two protons and two neutrons, the same as a helium nucleus.

Beta particle
An electron or positron (an electron with a positive electric charge) flung out by a decaying atom.

Control rod
A rod lowered into a nuclear reactor to absorb neutrons and slow down the nuclear reactions in the reactor or shut it down completely.

Fast reactor
A type of nuclear reactor that uses a mixture of uranium and plutonium fuel and produces nuclear fission by means of fast neutrons that have not been slowed down, as they are in a thermal reactor.

Gamma ray
A very short-wavelength electromagnetic wave given out by a nuclear reaction such as nuclear fission.

Heavy water
Deuterium oxide, water in which ordinary hydrogen has been replaced by the heavier hydrogen isotope deuterium.

Isotopes
Atoms of the same element that have different atomic weights because their nuclei contain different numbers of neutrons.

Light water
Ordinary water, H_2O.

Magnox
An early type of gas-cooled nuclear reactor.

Meltdown
A type of accident in which the fuel in a nuclear reactor overheats so much that it melts and may burn its way through the bottom of the reactor.

Moderator
A material inside a thermal reactor that slows down neutrons so that they are more likely to be absorbed and cause the fission of uranium-235 atoms.

Nuclear fission
Splitting a nucleus. Fission may happen naturally (spontaneous fission) or when a nucleus absorbs another particle (induced fission).

Nuclear fusion
A collision between two light nuclei which results in the two nuclei joining, or fusing, together to form a larger nucleus, usually with the release of some energy.

Nuclear radiation
Particles or electromagnetic waves given out by atomic nuclei.

Nuclear reactor
A device in which a controlled nuclear chain reaction takes place.

Nucleus
The particle or particles at the centre of an atom. Two types of particles are found in atomic nuclei – protons and neutrons.

Plutonium
A heavy silvery and highly radioactive element used as a fuel in some nuclear reactors and also to make nuclear weapons.

PWR
Pressurized water reactor, the most widely used type of thermal nuclear reactor.

Radioactive decay
A change in an atom's nucleus when it gives out radiation.

Reprocessing
The treatment of fuel from a nuclear reactor to separate the waste from material that can be used as fuel once again.

Tokamak
A type of experimental nuclear fusion reactor.

Turbine
A machine that uses the movement energy of a gas or liquid to spin a shaft.

Turbogenerator
An electricity generator driven by a turbine.

Uranium
A heavy element that is used as a fuel in nuclear reactors.

Books to read

Conserving Energy by Donna Bailey (Franklin Watts 1994)

Cycles in Science: Energy by Peter D. Riley (Heinemann Library, 1997)

Earthcare: Raw Materials by Miles Litvinoff (Heinemann Library, 1996)

Eyewitness Science: Energy by Jack Challoner (Dorling Kindersley and London Science Museum, 1993)

Nuclear Power by Nina Morgan (Wayland 1997)

Science Topics: Energy by Ann Fullick and Chris Oxlade (Heinemann Library, 1998)

Science Works: Energy by Steve Parker (Macdonald Young Books, 1995)

The Super Science Book of Energy by Jerry Wellington (Wayland, 1994)

The World's Energy Resources by Robin Kerrod (Wayland, 1994)

Power and energy consumption

Power is the measurement of how quickly energy is used. It is measured in joules per second, or watts. An electric iron might need 1,000 watts to work, but a portable radio might need only 10 watts. The energy needed to keep the radio going for one hour would run the iron for only six minutes, because the iron uses up energy ten times faster than the radio. The diagram to the right compares the power ratings of household electrical goods and of homes and power stations.

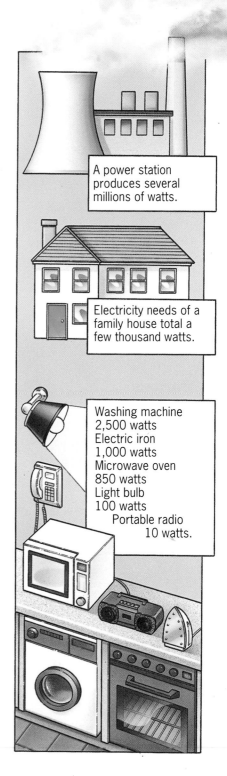

A power station produces several millions of watts.

Electricity needs of a family house total a few thousand watts.

Washing machine 2,500 watts
Electric iron 1,000 watts
Microwave oven 850 watts
Light bulb 100 watts
Portable radio 10 watts.

INDEX